JESUS
COMES
TO ME

Mary Terese Donze, A.S.C.

LIGUORI
PUBLICATIONS

**One Liguori Drive
Liguori, MO 63057-9999
(314) 464-2500**

Imprim Potest:
James Shea, C.SS.R.
Provincial, St. Louis Province
The Redemptorists

Imprimatur:
Monsignor Maurice F. Byrne
Vice Chancellor, Archdiocese of St. Louis

ISBN 0-89243-538-0
Library of Congress Catalog Number: 93-77239

Cover and interior art by Chris Sharp

May Jesus
in the holy Eucharist
be
loved, adored, honored, praised,
thanked, glorified, and trusted
by
all creatures
at
every moment
in
every tabernacle
throughout the whole world
until the end of time.
Amen.

Lovingly dedicated to
Saint Pius X,
who brought Christ back to
the little children

Contents

A Note to Parents, Grandparents, and Teachers

IF YOU ARE A PARENT, grandparent, or teacher who is helping a child prepare to receive his or her first holy Communion, you are blessed indeed. What greater privilege than to ready a child's heart to welcome for the first time the great and loving God!

Jesus Comes to Me is offered as a help in forming the child's mind and heart for that great event. While it can be used by the teacher in the formal instructions given before the child's first holy Communion, it is less structured than a manual and is meant more for use by a parent or grandparent or someone else in the home who is supplementing the teacher's instruction in the classroom.

Like its companion booklet, *Jesus Forgives My Sins*, this booklet is best read to the child in short sessions. The reading should take place in a warm, loving, and comfortable environment and at a time when the child seems most receptive. Read slowly, covering only a short section at a time, and give the child an opportunity to ask questions. The conversational tone of the booklet should lend itself to this manner of reading.

Before the first reading session with the child—and *Jesus Comes to Me* is written to be read directly from the page—be sure to read through the entire booklet yourself so you feel at ease with the text. This will help you anticipate where to expect the child to ask questions and where you may want to add comments of your own.

Some ideas expressed in the text may be difficult for the child—for any of us—to comprehend. Please do not omit them for that reason. Seeds of truth dropped into the child's heart will not be without fruit.

And because all the good we do for our children or for one another is not because of anything in ourselves but because God uses us as channels of his grace, beg the Holy Spirit to direct your words that they may touch the child's heart and nurture in him or her a growing desire for intimacy with Jesus.

May you be blessed in your endeavor.

Sister Mary Terese Donze

Jesus Is Here With Us

A LONG TIME AGO, people sometimes found it hard to pray because they had never seen God. In those days, it was harder to love God, too, because nobody knew what God looked like and nobody could tell anybody else how wonderful God was.

But God wanted very much for people to know and love him. So God sent Jesus from heaven. God let Jesus be born and grow up and walk around in a place called Palestine where all the people could see him. Then everybody would know what God looked like because Jesus IS God.

After that, it was easier to love God, too, because Jesus was right there in front of everybody. He looked just like any one of us and was very kind and loving to everyone.

But just because Jesus was like us, he died. Then, because he was God, too, he came alive again and went back to heaven. Only he did something very special before he went back to heaven. He took some bread and some wine and he blessed them and changed them into himself. He gave himself to his friends in the blessed bread and wine.

Jesus did more than that. He made it so all his priests could take bread and wine and do the same thing that he had done. That way, when he left for heaven, he would still be here with us in the blessed bread and blessed wine and we could receive him into our hearts. You will receive Jesus into your heart when you receive your first holy Communion and every other time after that when you allow him to come into your heart through the blessed bread and wine.

Jesus does this because he loves us. And when people love one another, they think of all sorts of ways of getting together. That is why Jesus changed some bread into himself so he could be inside us, near our hearts. It was like he loved us so much he just couldn't go back to heaven and leave us alone. Of course, we could read all about him and remember about him, but that wasn't enough for Jesus. He wanted to *stay* with us, be near us, have us talk with him, be friends.

Is it hard for you to understand that Jesus is still here with us, just as real as when he used to sit at the table and eat with his mother or when he went fishing on the lake with some friends or when he healed people and told sad people not to cry? If it seems hard to understand, that is because it *is* hard to understand. Your mommy and daddy think it is hard to understand, too. Even the priest finds it hard to understand how Jesus can still be with us like he was with the people a long time ago.

But we don't let it worry us that it is hard to understand because we all love Jesus and we *believe* what he says. We know he can be in the blessed bread and blessed wine because he told us it was so. Jesus is God and can do things like that.

God just has to say something, and it happens. It is like when Jesus said to a sick man, "Get well." And the man stood up and got well. And Jesus said to the wind, "Stop blowing." And it stopped blowing right in the middle of a storm. Jesus even told a dead man to come alive, and the man sat up and started talking just as if he didn't remember that he had been dead. God's words are never just words; they make things happen.

When Jesus changed the bread and wine into himself many years ago, he was thinking about us, too. He already knew our names at that time, and he was thinking about how someday we would learn about him and love him. He wanted to be here still when that time came. He wanted to be here in a way that would let us be close to him the way people want to be when they love each other. So Jesus changed the bread into himself. Then he could come right into our hearts and not just stay outside of us and maybe put his arms around us.

Jesus keeps changing bread into himself at every Mass. It is wonderful. It is so wonderful that nobody but God could have figured out how to do it. But it is true. And each time we look up to the altar at Mass and see the blessed bread, what we *see*—the bread—is not really there. What we *don't see*—Jesus—is really there. Of course, without the bread Jesus would not be there. But Jesus isn't the bread. It is like a violin making music. Without the violin, the music would not be there. But the violin is not the music. It is something like that with Jesus and the bread.

Jesus Makes Us Like Himself

MAYBE YOU ARE THINKING, *How can Jesus be in a small piece of bread? How can he make himself so tiny and squeeze himself into a little piece of food?* But that is not the way it is at all. Jesus does not make himself little and hide inside the piece of bread. Jesus just uses the bread as a way to bring himself inside us where he can be close to our hearts. But the bread still looks like bread and smells like bread and tastes like bread. And when you eat it, it will feed your body and become part of your body like the other food you eat does.

But while your body is changing the bread part into you and helping you to keep on living and growing stronger, Jesus, the true holy Bread, is feeding your soul. It is like you remember you have a body and a soul. Our bodies need food. Food gives life to our bodies. Our soul needs food, too. Jesus is the food that gives life to our souls. When he comes to us in holy Communion, he lets us share in his God-life by feeding our souls with his Godness. Only, instead of our souls making Jesus *a part of ourselves* like our bodies do with food, Jesus makes us *a part of himself*. He makes us more and more like God.

Every time we receive the blessed bread and blessed wine, we get more and more like Jesus. A man named Saint Paul, who knew all about this and who loved Jesus very much, once said, "I live. No, not I. But Christ lives in me." It was like Jesus had been with Paul so many times that he had changed Paul into being like himself. Paul really was still Paul, but he was so much like Jesus that he almost forgot about Paul. And Paul liked it that way because to be like Jesus is the way to be your very best self, every bit of you.

Why Jesus Chose Bread and Wine

MAYBE YOU WONDER why Jesus used bread and wine instead of something like Oreo cookies and a Kool-Aid drink. One reason, for sure, is that there weren't any Oreo cookies and Kool-Aid drinks when Jesus lived in Palestine.

Maybe another reason Jesus used bread is that bread is something common and everybody knows what you are talking about when you say "bread." And there is this about bread, too: no matter if you have it at every meal, you never really get tired of it like you might get tired of chili or something like that if you had it at every meal.

Besides, there is something special about bread. As far back as anybody can remember, people have always been eating bread. Sometimes bread was the only food poor people had to keep themselves alive. And because it kept them alive, people began to be careful with bread and to treat it with respect. It used to be that some bakers would never turn their backs to the oven while bread was baking because of the great respect they had for God's gift of bread that kept them alive. Or if they dropped a piece of bread on the ground, they would kiss it when they picked it up to show how sorry they were for not being careful with the bread. Children used to be taught that if they found some bread on the ground, they should pick it up and put it on a fence post for the birds.

Jesus himself must have thought bread was something special, too. When he taught us to pray, he told us to say, "Give us this day our daily bread." It was like he knew we would want hamburgers and pizzas and ice cream and things like that, but he called all food "bread" because it is what keeps us alive.

Wine is like bread. Everybody knows about it, and they don't get tired of it. We know that is true because people drank wine almost as long ago as the time when Adam and Eve were living, and people are still drinking it.

Wine is not like other things people drink. It is not like orange juice or lemonade or hot chocolate. They always taste like orange juice or lemonade or hot chocolate. But there are ever so many kinds of wine, and each wine has a different taste. Different kinds of wine have different colors, too. Some are white, and some are red or pink. Some are as golden as honey. Dark wines look almost black.

Wine has something special about it, too, just

like bread. A long time ago, some people who didn't know about the true God looked at the red wine and thought that it was like the red life-giving blood in their veins. So they pretended that this beautiful wine was the blood of their make-believe god. They offered it to their pretend god, and then they drank the lovely red wine and hoped they would get to be like a god.

Jesus knew all these stories about bread and wine and that they were special. Maybe that was why he chose bread and wine to change into himself. Or maybe Jesus chose bread and wine because it made him think of how he was going to die on the cross for us. A grain of wheat is put into the ground and dies before  it can grow into many grains of wheat that will be crushed to make flour for bread. And grapes have to be pressed and mashed before they can become wine. In that same way, Jesus had to die like a grain of wheat, and his blood was poured out like the juice of the grapes.

There might have been still another reason Jesus chose to use bread and wine to give us himself. One loaf of bread is made up of many grains of wheat, and it takes many grapes to make one cup of wine. So when Jesus took bread and said, "This is my body" and took a cup of wine and said, "This is my blood," then changed them into himself, maybe he was thinking of how he wants all of us to be united in him and with one another into one family of God, just like many grains of wheat unite to make one loaf and many grapes go together to make one glass of wine.

You Are Part
of Jesus' Family

SOON YOU ARE going
to celebrate your first
holy Communion. That
means that Jesus will
come into your heart
in a way he has never
come before, in a way
he hopes he may come
many, many times
after that. He will
come to you in a small

bit of blessed bread and maybe in a small sip of
blessed wine.

You were not allowed to do this before because you were too little to know how the blessed
bread and blessed wine are really Jesus. It is like
when you were a baby and could not sit at the
table with the grownups and eat the food they
ate. You sat in a highchair and ate baby food.
Now that you are bigger, you sit right at the table

and eat the same food the rest of the family eats, and it makes you feel more like a part of the family.

When you celebrate holy Communion, you will go to the altar just like the grownups, and you will receive Jesus just like they do. That means that you, too, are growing up and becoming a part of the bigger family that we call the parish and of the still bigger family that we call the Church. And when we talk about the Church, we do not mean the building where we go to Mass but all the people who believe about Jesus as we do.

Get Your Heart Ready for Jesus

COMING TO BE with Jesus in holy Communion is like being invited to a party—his party. And usually when we go to a party, we take a gift. Our gift to Jesus is the bread and wine that we offer at the Mass. Maybe you didn't bring the bread and wine, but somebody did. And it counts as a gift from all of us to Jesus.

In the Mass, Jesus changes our gifts into himself and then gives them back to us so that all of us can share in him and feel like we are all his brothers and sisters.

Even if many people go to holy Communion, we all receive Jesus. It is not like Jesus walks around at the party and maybe doesn't notice some people and skips over them because there are so many people there. Sometimes that happens at other people's parties. But not with Jesus. No, he comes to each one who takes the blessed bread. And in his own way, he lets each of us know how special we are to him.

Since Jesus is coming to you in holy Communion, you will want to get your heart ready for him. When you have company at home, your parents clean up the house and maybe put some flowers on the table and get out the good dishes. In just the same way, you will want to do something to get ready for Jesus to come into your heart.

When Saint Therese was a little girl getting ready to celebrate her first holy Communion, she started a long time before to make her heart ready for Jesus. She knew we don't put out the best dishes for Jesus or give him real flowers, but she thought how she could make something like a garden in her heart. Each time she said "I love you, Jesus" or was kind to somebody for Jesus' sake or did what her mother told her to do without fussing about it, it was as if she put a beautiful flower into her heart-garden.

Then the day before she celebrated her first holy Communion, Saint Therese went to the Sacrament of Penance and was sorry for her sins and told them to the priest. She wanted her heart to be clean and free from sin when Jesus came to her, just like we make our house clean for company. After that, since she was all ready, Saint Therese could hardly wait for Jesus to come.

The next morning when she went to Mass, she remembered how her heart was full of lovely flowers. She was going to offer them all to Jesus. But when it was time and she walked up to the altar to receive Jesus in holy Communion, she forgot all about her heart-garden and the flowers. All she could think about was Jesus being right there for her. "I love you, Jesus," she kept telling him over and over. "And I give myself to you forever." Although Saint Therese had forgotten about the flowers, Jesus knew about them, and he was pleased that she had done that for him.

Saint Therese received Jesus in holy Communion many times after that, but she always remembered to get her heart ready for him by telling him she loved him and by being kind to everybody and by doing what her mother and father told her to do without pouting and putting up a big fuss.

Your First Communion Day

BY THE TIME the day comes for you to receive your first holy Communion, maybe you will have a heart-garden full of beautiful flowers for Jesus, too. You can start right now or any time. Then, on the day before your first holy Communion, you may want to go to the Sacrament of Penance like Saint Therese did so Jesus can forgive all your sins. Then your heart will be even more ready for him the next day when he will come so specially.

When it is time for you to receive Jesus in holy Communion, fold your hands and walk up to the altar where the priest is standing. Then lay your left hand open on top of your right

hand like this (show the child) and wait until the priest or the Communion minister places the blessed bread—we sometimes call it the sacred host—into your hand and says to you, "The Body of Christ." That is to remind you that this is not just a piece of ordinary bread. It is truly Jesus, who is God. You think of that and you say, "Amen." That means you understand about Jesus and welcome him and invite him into your heart.

After you have received the sacred bread, step to the side a bit and pick up the blessed bread with your right hand and put it in your mouth and eat it like Jesus said we should. While you eat this blessed bread, think of how Jesus has come to be inside you—just that close!—and how he is putting more and more of his own Godness into you so that, little by little, you will become more like him.

When you get back to your place, close your eyes for a little while so you can think about Jesus better. Thank him for coming to you. Tell him how much you love him and how wonderful you think he is. Then you might want to ask him to bless you and your family and poor children all over the world. Tell him anything that makes you happy, too—like how you and some kids at school won a ball game or how the teacher put a gold star on your spelling paper. And if there is any-thing that makes you feel sad—like maybe how hard it is to learn to read or how your dog got lost or somebody you love is sick—you can talk to Jesus about that, too. You can say anything you want to him because at holy Communion time, Jesus is there *just for you*. After a while, if every-body starts to sing, sing along with them. That is another good way to show Jesus that you thank him not only for coming to you but for coming to everybody else, too.

Some people say that their first holy Com-munion day was the happiest day of their lives. They felt very wonderful, and they will never forget it. But don't feel sad if after you receive Jesus in holy Communion, you don't feel a bit different than you did before. That happens to a lot of people, too. If we could really *see* Jesus, it would be easier, of course. But we live by *believ-ing* in Jesus, and sometimes just believing doesn't make us feel as happy as we thought we would feel. That is all right.

If you don't feel different after receiving holy Communion, you can tell Jesus that, too. He will understand, and it won't matter to him. He will love you just the same and be very happy to be in your heart. More than that, Jesus will be wanting you to come to him often in holy Communion, even if it doesn't make you feel different. The thing that matters for you and for Jesus is that, little by little, Jesus will make you more and more like himself.

Because it is such a special day for you, you may get presents or a cake on your first Commun-ion day. That will be lots of fun. But maybe once in a while during the day you will want to remem-ber about Jesus and how he came to you. If you do, you can say some loving things to him in your heart. You won't have to stop what you are doing and look solemn or act like you are in church. You can talk to Jesus in your heart even when you are eating a big piece of chocolate cake or doing anything else.

When your first holy Communion day is over, try to receive Jesus into your heart as many days as you can. Once Jesus has been within you in this special way, he keeps hoping you will invite him again and again. Nobody, *just nobody*, will ever love you so much and for all the time like Jesus does. And nothing makes him more happy than when you love him, too.

God bless you!

Some Practical Considerations

- If the child is part of a class that will receive holy Communion as a group in which there are dress regulations, help the child to regard the dress-up element as another way of doing something special for Jesus rather than merely as dressing up for its own sake.
- Should you plan to give the child a gift in remembrance of his or her first holy Communion, make the gift as related as possible to the occasion: a child's book of prayers, a rosary, a colorful book of the saints, a decorative blessed candle that can be lighted at the family meal and on other special celebrations in the child's life. (If the child is going to get a bicycle, a doll, a gift of money, or something similar, let it be on some other occasion than on first Communion day.)

- On occasion of the child's future reception of the Eucharist, spend some time speaking with him or her in an informal way about these visits with Jesus. It may be just a sentence or two that you say the evening before or as the child leaves for church. Do all you can to make the child's repeated reception of the sacrament something to be prepared for and cherished so that it will never become a meaningless routine. During a drive through the countryside, you might want to point out to the child a field of ripening wheat. Some of that wheat may someday become the body of Jesus—Jesus himself—in holy Communion.

- You may also want to show the child a grape arbor when the grapes are ripe and hanging in clusters from the vine and make some relevant observation. A word here or there, done naturally but with the intent of helping the child find God everywhere, will not be without its blessing from heaven.

- Remember that your own example and the reverence and frequency with which you approach the Eucharist will be the greatest factor in influencing the child's attitude toward this most sublime sacrament.

The End

MORE BY SISTER TERESE DONZE...

Jesus Forgives My Sins

Get involved in your child's religious education. Supplement his or her formal preparation for the Sacrament of Penance with this booklet designed to encourage family discussion and celebration of this milestone in your child's Catholic faith life. *$2.95*

I Can Pray the Rosary!

In this booklet, each of the mysteries—Joyful, Sorrowful, and Glorious—is simply explained in easy-to-understand language. Sister Donze has illustrated this booklet herself and includes instructions for praying the rosary and a section of prayers. *$3.95*
Bilingual (English/Spanish) edition—I Can Pray the Rosary!/Puedo Rezar el Rosario! *$2.95*

I Can Pray About Anything!

This addition to Sister Donze's bestselling *I Can Pray...* series contains more than 40 prayers for children in pre-K through grade 3. Each prayer is meant primarily for an adult to read and pray with preschoolers to teach them that they can pray about anything in their lives. *$3.95*

I Can Pray With the Saints!

Thirteen simple biographies highlight a virtue or quality that made the saint portrayed so special. Each sketch ends with a prayer, helping children thank Jesus for giving them such a good role model to follow. *$3.95*
Bilingual (English/Spanish) edition—I Can Pray With the Saints!/Puedo Rezar Con los Saints! *$2.95*

Order from your local bookstore or write
Liguori Publications
Box 060, Liguori, MO 63057-9999
Please add 15% to your total for shipping and handling
($3.50 minimum, $15 maximum).